ALL the MAMMALS in the WORLD

David Opie

PETER PAUPER PRESS, INC.
RYE BROOK, NEW YORK

The author would like to thank Wayt Gibbs
for his feedback on an early draft of this book.

Published by Peter Pauper Press, Inc.
3 International Drive
Rye Brook, New York 10573 USA

Library of Congress Cataloging-in-Publication Data

Names: Opie, David, author, illustrator.
Title: All the mammals in the world / David Opie.
Description: First edition. | Rye Brook, New York : Peter Pauper Press,
Inc., 2023. | Audience: Ages 3-8 | Audience: Grades K-1 | Summary:
"Explore the vast world of mammals led by your very own prehistoric tour
guide, a Morganucodon. Affectionately nicknamed by some as "Morgie," a
Morganucodon was an early primitive mammal that lived over 200 million
years ago. Join this little Morgie as it discovers just how wide the
world of mammals is-from tiny mice, huge blue whales, and dolphins, to
groundhogs, gorillas, and even people!"-- Provided by publisher.
Identifiers: LCCN 2022050378 | ISBN 9781441335593 (hardcover)
Subjects: LCSH: Mammals--Juvenile literature.
Classification: LCC QL706.2 .O65 2023 | DDC 599--dc23/eng/20221027
LC record available at https://lccn.loc.gov/2022050378

ISBN 978-1-4413-3559-3
Manufactured for Peter Pauper Press, Inc.
Printed in China

7 6 5 4 3 2 1

Visit us at www.peterpauper.com

Mammals developed slowly from reptile-like animals
about 200 million years ago,
not long after dinosaurs began their reign on Earth.
The earliest mammals,
like the now-extinct Morganucodon (mor-GAN-ew-ko-don) pictured here,
looked a little like modern mice.
They had fur, were mostly active at night,
and had different types of teeth,
which helped them chew every tasty morsel of the insects they ate.
Unlike most mammals living today, they probably laid eggs.

"I wonder what mammals look like now?"

Most mammals have a warm, steady body temperature,
are covered in fur,
have specialized teeth,
a sharp sense of hearing,
and a big brain compared to the rest of their body.
The majority of mammal mothers give birth to live babies,
and feed their babies with milk.

Mammals have spread to just about every place on the planet.
They run, hop, climb, burrow, gallop, glide, fly, and swim.

"You're mammals, too?"

The most common type of mammal today is the rodent,
known for gnawing with front teeth that never stop growing.
Mice, voles, rats, squirrels, chipmunks, porcupines, muskrats,
lemmings, groundhogs, gophers, and chinchillas are all rodents.

Beavers are large rodents.
They use their sharp teeth
to chew down trees and branches in order to build
their own wetland neighborhood of dams and lodges.
The biggest rodent is the capybara,
twice as big as the beaver.

"Hey, you look familiar!"

Many mammals climb through the tree canopy,
and some, like flying squirrels, sugar gliders,
colugos, and feathertail gliders,
have folds of skin
that they can unfurl like a magical cape
and sail away!

The second most common mammal type is the bat,
the only mammal that can flap its wings
and fly like a bird.
Bats tend to spend their days
roosting in caves, trees, and old buildings.
Most bats hunt insects at night.
Some bats, like the flying foxes,
eat mainly fruit and flowers.
One of the world's smallest mammals is the bumblebee bat,
which is not much bigger than an actual bumblebee.

"I like eating tiny insects at night, too! Maybe they got that from me!"

And what about BIG mammals?
The elephant is a huge mammal
that grows so tall,
it wouldn't fit in most kids' bedrooms.
And the giraffe is almost twice as tall as an elephant.
Bison are giant mammals that thunder across the plains,
and camels can pop their heads way up
to gaze across the far-spreading desert sands.

The hippopotamus and rhinoceros
each weigh as much as a car,
and the brown bear can rear up on its hind legs,
and tower over almost everyone else.

"All these giants evolved from little creatures like me?"

And the biggest of all animals
to have ever lived on Earth—past and present—
is the blue whale!

Some mammals live in the water,
like dolphins, porpoises, orcas, narwhals,
and of course many other types of whales.
But they have to surface
from time to time
to breathe air,
while fish can stay underwater.

Most mammals can swim if they must,
to escape from flood waters or predators.
Some mammals, like hippopotamuses, sea lions,
seals, otters, platypuses, beavers, and walruses
are strong swimmers and
live much of their lives underwater.
Dugongs and manatees stay in the water
and don't walk around on land.
But they all have to come up for air occasionally, too.

Almost all mammals give birth to live babies,
but echidnas and duck-billed platypuses
still lay eggs like their ancient ancestors—
and like Morganucodons, 200 million years ago.

"You lay eggs,
just like me!"

Some mammals—called marsupials—
give birth to tiny, frail babies
which then climb into their mother's pouch,
where they find protection and milk
as they continue to grow.

Kangaroos, wombats, opossums,
wallabies, koalas,
Tasmanian devils, and bandicoots
all belong to this group.

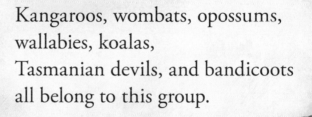

"It looks warm and cozy
in that kangaroo pouch."

Mammals are not nearly as colorful
as birds and fish can be.
Mostly, their fur colors and patterns
help them blend into their surroundings:
white fur in snowy places,
and earthy colors to hide in forests,
rocks, and grass.
There are some exceptions,
like the flashy zebra
that has bold black and white stripes.
Scientists think the stripes confuse predators,
protect the zebras from pesky flies,
and help them stay cool.

"I'm good at
hiding, too."

Primates are a large group of mammals
that includes apes, monkeys, lemurs, tarsiers,
bush babies, and lorises.
Most primates adapted to living in trees,
so they usually have strong hands, fingers, and thumbs
for grabbing branches and vines.
They are smart and have big brains
compared to the rest of their bodies.

"So, is that ALL
the mammals that
have developed
over the last 200
million years?"

People are primates, and therefore mammals, too!
Humans have done some amazing things.
They've walked on the Moon, explored the depths of the oceans,
and sent spacecraft to investigate neighboring planets and beyond.
They make art and communicate in many different languages.

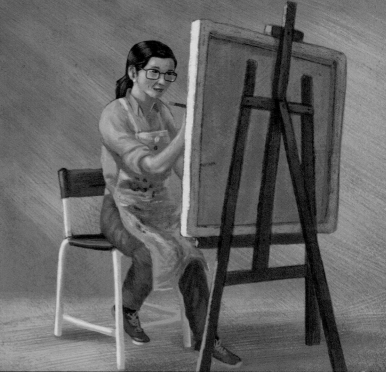

They invented complicated machines, like cars
that zip along highways stretching around the continents.
They've built huge, sprawling cities, cleared vast forests,
and transformed billions of acres of land into farms.
Humans affect the air, the water, the land, and the climate.
People are part of the natural world,
and they depend on its health to survive.

"Mammals sure have come a
long way in 200 million years!"

From tiny mice
to huge blue whales,
to the dolphins and porpoises swimming in the oceans,
to the people on every continent,
to groundhogs and prairie dogs burrowing underground,
to flying squirrels gliding through the forest canopy,
to bats winging across the night sky,
we all share the same home planet.

"And we're all in this together!"

A Note from the Author

Mammals are certainly an interesting group of animals, and I'm not just saying that because I am one (and so are you). Although there are only about 6,000 identified species of mammals—compared to more than 33,000 species of fish, and 10,000 different types of birds—there's a huge range within that group. There are small bats flying at night that use echolocation to scoop up bugs. There are beavers busily building elaborate systems of dams to create their own watery habitat. There are blue whales (the largest of all animals) sweeping their way across the wide oceans, and there are even humans, studying, reflecting, writing, and creating artwork about this vast group.

A major reason I wanted to write this book is to remind the reader that humans are animals too. We are very much part of the natural world. It can be easy to forget since we spend so much time inside.

We humans have shaped much of the world that we now experience. As we've expanded our "footprint" on the Earth, we have affected the planet in many ways. We have changed the air, water, and land.

By burning massive amounts of fossil fuels (which releases heat-capturing greenhouse gases into the atmosphere), and by cutting down forests (to clear land for farming, real estate development, and to make wood products), we humans have upset our planet's temperature balance. As a result, average global temperatures are rising, which has caused many problems: Ice sheets and glaciers are melting, sea levels are rising, storms are getting stronger and more destructive in some areas, droughts are affecting other regions, coral reefs are bleaching and dying, forest fires are getting worse, and animals are losing their habitats.

We humans must act to stop these problems that we've caused, and make our planet a safe place for all living creatures. Here are some resources to find out about these important issues:

https://climatekids.nasa.gov
https://climatekids.ca
https://www.un.org/sustainabledevelopment/climate-action-superheroes/
https://ec.europa.eu/clima/sites/youth/
www.worldwildlife.org
www.iucn.org

About Morganucodon

The main character in this book is a type of Morganucodon, which is sometimes referred to as a "proto-mammal." "Proto-" means "original" or "primitive." They show a link between their lizard-like ancestors and what we think of today as true mammals. For example, Morganucodons had fur, specialized teeth, and increasing brain size (compared to the rest of the body), but they didn't have the tiny bones that make up the inner ears of present-day mammals, and they probably didn't have the higher, constant body temperature of modern mammals. They were very successful animals, and their fossilized remains have been found in Wales,

China, Europe, and North America. They really got around!

T.S. Kemp's book *Mammals: A Very Short Introduction* summarizes the evolution of animals called synapsids as they slowly developed into mammals. The mammalian characteristics build up and lead to Morganucodons. The author states that Morganucodons represent "a new kind of animal." Although Morganucodons are not the direct ancestors of mammals, relatives of this "new" animal have gone on to develop into the huge range of creatures covered in these pages.

Glossary

echolocation: The process some animals use to detect the position of other animals and objects. Animals that use echolocation, like bats and dolphins, make a sound and can locate objects by the way that sound bounces back.

fossil fuel: A power source made from decomposing plants and animals. Examples are coal, oil, and natural gas.

glacier: A large mass of ice made from tightly packed snow. Glaciers form over many years and move very slowly.

greenhouse gas: A type of gas that can trap heat inside the Earth's atmosphere, just like the glass walls of a greenhouse. Carbon dioxide and methane are greenhouse gases.

predator: An animal that hunts and eats other animals.

synapsid: A group of animals that includes the ancestors that mammals developed from.

wetland: An area of land that is soaked with water, like marshes and swamps.

(Left to right): Little brown bat, spinner dolphin

Identification

Cover

1. Slow loris
2. Orangutan
3. North American porcupine
4. Pygmy three-toed sloth
5. Chipmunk
6. Koala
7. Red squirrel
8. Red panda
9. Giraffe

10. Flying squirrel
11. Virginia opossum
12. Ring-tailed lemur
13. Tarsier
14. Squirrel monkey
15. Eastern gray squirrel
16. Raccoon
17. Bottlenose dolphins
18. Beaver

19. Humpback whale
20. California sea lions
21. Echidna
22. River otter
23. Lion
24. Eastern barred bandicoot
25. Vampire bat
26. Moose
27. Groundhog

28. Mandrill
29. Eastern cottontail rabbit
30. Red fox
31. Morganucodon
32. Zebra
33. Common marmoset
34. Kangaroo
35. Armadillo
36. African elephant

Animals are not necessarily to scale.

Page 1   Morganucodon

Pages 2-3   The dinosaur is based on a Dracoraptor, and is not a mammal. Morganucodon is below.

Pages 4-5   Theropod dinosaur (not a mammal), Morganucodon, and beetle (not a mammal)

Page 6   (Top, left to right) Musk ox, cheetah, (middle) prairie dogs, (bottom) lion, fennec fox

Page 7   (Top, left to right) Bobcat nursing kittens, horse, kangaroo, (middle) common pipistrelle bat, flying fox, flying squirrel, squirrel monkey, (lower left, top to bottom) bottlenose dolphins, California sea lion, (right) German shepherd dog, house cat, Morganucodon

Page 8   (Top) Muskrat, groundhog, prairie dog, (middle) eastern gray squirrel, woodland vole, chinchilla, chipmunk, kangaroo rat, (bottom) crested porcupine, paca, Norway lemming

Page 9   (Top) beavers, (middle) capybaras, (bottom) brown rat, wood mouse, Morganucodon

Page 10-11

1. Philippine colugo
2. Flying squirrel
3. Flying squirrel
4. Sugar glider
5. Flying squirrel
6. Indian giant flying squirrel
7. Philippine colugo
8. Sugar glider
9. Flying squirrel
10. Morganucodon

Page 12-13

1. Pallid bat
2. Egyptian fruit bat
3. Giant golden-crowned flying fox
4. Giant golden-crowned flying fox
5. Vampire bat
6. Brown long-eared bat
7. Townsend's big-eared bat
8. Little brown bat
9. Pipistrelle bat
10. Mexican free-tailed bat
11. Bumblebee bat
12. Lesser long-nosed bat
13. Morganucodon

Animals are not necessarily to scale.
Some animals in the background are not identified.

Page 14-15   (From left to right) Giraffe, Bactrian camel, rhinoceros, hippopotamus, bison, brown bear, African elephant, Morganucodon

Page 16-17   Blue whale, Morganucodon

Page 18-19

1. Bottlenose dolphin
2. Harbor porpoise
3. Morganucodon
4. Orca
5. Bottlenose dolphin
6. Narwhal
7. Amazon river dolphin
8. Humpback whales
9. Beluga whale
10. Minke whale
11. Spinner dolphins
12. Spinner dolphin
13. Bottlenose dolphin
14. Sperm whale
15. Right whale
16. Bowhead whale
17. Blainville's beaked whale

Page 20-21

1. Platypus
2. Beaver
3. Morganucodon
4. Atlantic walrus
5. California sea lion
6. Dugong
7. California sea lion
8. River otter
9. Hippopotamus
10. Beaver
11. Manatees

Page 22   (top) Echidna, (bottom) Morganucodon, platypus

Page 23

Koala

Virginia opossum

Morganucodon

Kangaroo

Wombat

Tasmanian devil

Eastern barred bandicoot

Page 24 (top)   (left to right) Arctic hare, arctic fox, polar bear, arctic ermine

Page 24 (bottom)

Red squirrel

Moose

Virginia opossum

Raccoon

Black bear

Coyote

Red fox

Deer mouse

White-tailed deer

Groundhog

Chipmunk

Rabbit

Animals are not necessarily to scale.
Some animals in the background are not identified.

Tiger

Lion

Spotted hyena

Cheetah

Ethiopian wolf

Gazelle

Zebra

Morganucodon

Ring-tailed lemur

Spider monkey

Capuchin monkey

Tarsier

Macaque

Western lowland gorilla

Mandrill

Common marmoset

Chimpanzee

Gibbon

Golden lion tamarin

Morganucodon

Page 28   (Top) Astronauts on the Moon, (middle, from left) California sea lion, human divers, (bottom left) Egyptian sculpture of Nefertiti from around 1345 BCE, (bottom right) person painting

Page 29   (Top) City scene, (bottom) corn farm, farmers with dairy cows, (on stump) Morganucodon

Page 30-31

Red squirrel

Tarsier

Virginia opossum

Squirrel monkey

Vampire bat

Koala

Giant golden-crowned flying fox

Flying squirrel

African elephant

Humpback whale

Morganucodon

Blue whale

Harbor porpoises

Bottlenose dolphins

Bactrian camel

Moose

Kangaroo

Zebra

Red fox

Tiger

Human

Polar bear

Chipmunk

Giant panda

Armadillo

Mandrill

Prairie dogs

Fennec fox

Rabbit

Wood mouse

Groundhog

Wild boar

Animals are not necessarily to scale.